£7.99

ISBN: 978-1-907823-50-3

Images © Corbis.com and Shutterstock.com

A Pillar Box Red Publication

we ❤ love you...

Harry Styles

A 2014 ANNUAL

Written by Sarah Milne
Designed by Duncan Cook

CONTENTS

From the Beginning

Harry Edward Styles was born on February 1 1994, the younger child of Anne and Des, and brother to older sister Gemma. Harry and his family grew up in Holmes Chapel, a small but pretty village in Cheshire - Manchester was their nearest city, which is around 20 miles away.

He had a happy childhood, his parents divorced when he was seven but his mum remarried to Robin, his stepdad.

At school, Harry was always a joker, and liked to have fun and create havoc wherever he went. School friend Will Sweeney, who formed the band White Eskimo with Harry while they were just 15, says that they loved to walk around the place acting like idiots in public - they once got told off in posh supermarket Waitrose for shouting 'bogies' as loud as they could.

And it seems that Harry was always a hit with the ladies. Another old school friend, Nick Clough - also a member of White Eskimo, said: "He was always really popular with girls. He had a lot of girlfriends through our school years. None of them said no to him." But Nick also reveals a more romantic side to Harry, saying that whenever Harry had a

Holmes Chapel

girlfriend he would "get them flowers and take them for meals. He used to cook candlelit dinners and give them gifts."

And, despite being quite shy initially, once Harry got up on stage with the band White Eskimo, his confidence grew - he loved performing and shaking his tambourine at an audience of (mainly) screaming schoolgirls. Friends from that time say that Harry always had a star quality about him, and as soon as they knew he was auditioning for the X Factor that he'd go far.

White Eskimo

he worked part-time in a local bakery, and since he's found fame has popped back to see the ladies he used to work alongside, joking that one of them used to pinch his bum on a Saturday! He still stays close to his school friends, and sees them as much as his busy schedule will allow. His family are his number one priority, and he still texts his mum up to five times a day.

When Harry decided to audition for the X Factor as a solo artist, his life was about to change forever…

As well as his fun-loving personality, Harry has always been loyal to his friends and family - before the X Factor,

W. Manderville
GROCER & BAKER
MAKER OF
HOVIS

TELE

Fact File

Name: Harry Edward Styles.

Date of birth: 1st February 1994.

Starsign: Aquarius - this means Harry should be independent, creative and loyal. On the other hand, Aquarians can also be stubborn and unpredictable!

Hometown: Holmes Chapel, a beautiful village in Cheshire.

Lives: Harry now lives in London, and used to share with band mate Louis.

Family: Mum Anne and dad Des, older sister Gemma and Stepdad Robin.

Hair: Brown.

Eyes: Green / blue.

Shoe size: 10.5.

Height: 5ft 10 inches.

School nickname: Hazza.

Likes: Animals (especially turtles), Manchester United, sweetcorn and his mum (aahh).

Dislikes: Swearing, snakes, olives and beetroot.

Favourite song: 'Free Falling' by John Mayer.

Further facts:

1. Harry's favourite TV show is Family Guy.

2. The first gig Harry ever attended was Nickelback in Manchester.

3. Harry cites David Hasselhoff as one of his biggest heroes.

4. Harry secretly loves chick flicks and his favourite movies are Love Actually, Titanic and The Notebook.

5. It was Harry who came up with the band name One Direction.

Guzzler Panama – Anagram Puzzle

Below are eight anagrams all linked to Harry. Can you guess what each one is? So you're not kept 'Up All Night' guessing, there is a clue for each one.

1. Oriented Icon ___ _____

    Clue: Harry is a member of this.

2. Dear Shrewdly Stray _____ _____ _____

    Clue: Harry was named this when he was born.

3. Hail Curry _____ ____

    Clue: This trademark is almost as famous as he is.

4. Yum Or Volume ____ ____ ___

    Clue: Harry makes no secret of his special relationship with this family member and he'd tell you to do this.

5. Curve Yet ____ ____

    Clue: He shares this description with fluffy kittens and the rest of One Direction.

6. Oh Cheap Smell _____ _____

    Clue: They say it's where the heart is, so Harry's must be here.

7. Lazily Manuals Oil In ____ _____ _____ ____

    Clue: He wouldn't be without them. (In any order)

8. Guy Toe Boot ___ __ __ ___

    Clue: What we'd all like to hear Harry singing to us.

Answers on page 60.

THE START of 1D

When Harry Edward Styles stood in the queue for the X Factor 2010 auditions to perform as a solo artist, there's no way he could have imagined what would happen to him by the end of the competition. Harry, along with the other boys – Zayn, Louis, Liam and Niall, all impressed the judges at their first audition, and they made it through to the final stages of boot camp. Harry sang a cover of Stevie Wonder's song 'Isn't She Lovely' at his first audition, all the judges apart from Louis thought he had a great voice.

Mr Walsh changed his mind when Harry sang the Oasis hit 'Stop Crying Your Heart Out' at bootcamp.

Disappointingly, they were all rejected at this point, and denied the chance to go through to the judges' houses in the 'boys' category. But something about all five of them had made an impression and guest judge Nicole Scherzinger suggested forming them into a boy band for the 'groups' category.

Thrown together, the boys were shocked to have been given a second chance. After the initial excitement, there was much work to be done - the boys had just five weeks to turn themselves from solo artists into a band! At one point the boys moved into a house at the bottom of Harry's stepfather's garden.

Then Harry came up with the name One Direction, mainly

14

in over the previous months was not going to waste - they were certain they would carry on as a group and try to find success on their own.

And find success they did - in January 2011, they signed a £2 million record contract with Simon Cowell's label Syco. The rest of 2011 just got better, with singles and their first album released, as well as their first sellout tour - Up All Night.

because he thought it would sound cool when the X Factor announcer said it in his deep voice. The rest of the boys loved it, and it stuck. They were finally on the way to becoming a band.

Since then, the boys have cracked America, released their second album, 'Take Me Home' and released a documentary film 'This Is Us.' There's no denying that One Direction are the biggest boy band around.

During the live shows, we really started to see Harry's personality shine through. He was given the task of being house 'mole' for the Xtra Factor spin-off show, where he had to report on housemates secrets - it was clear he loved being in front of the camera and had a good sense of humour. It was great to see the boys develop such a strong bond - remember it had only been a few months since they met!

But being famous brings with it a lot of attention, and Harry, as well as the other boys, can often be found in the newspapers, being photographed with famous friends, or supposed new girlfriends, or being mobbed by fans. The most important thing is that he still loves what he does, and he is having fun doing it. Long may it continue!

The live shows had their ups and downs for One Direction, but in general, they were given good feedback, and their faithful fans now known as 'Directioners', were growing every week. When they made it through to the final three, everyone was disappointed to see them come third. The boys were obviously gutted to have lost, but the hard work they'd put

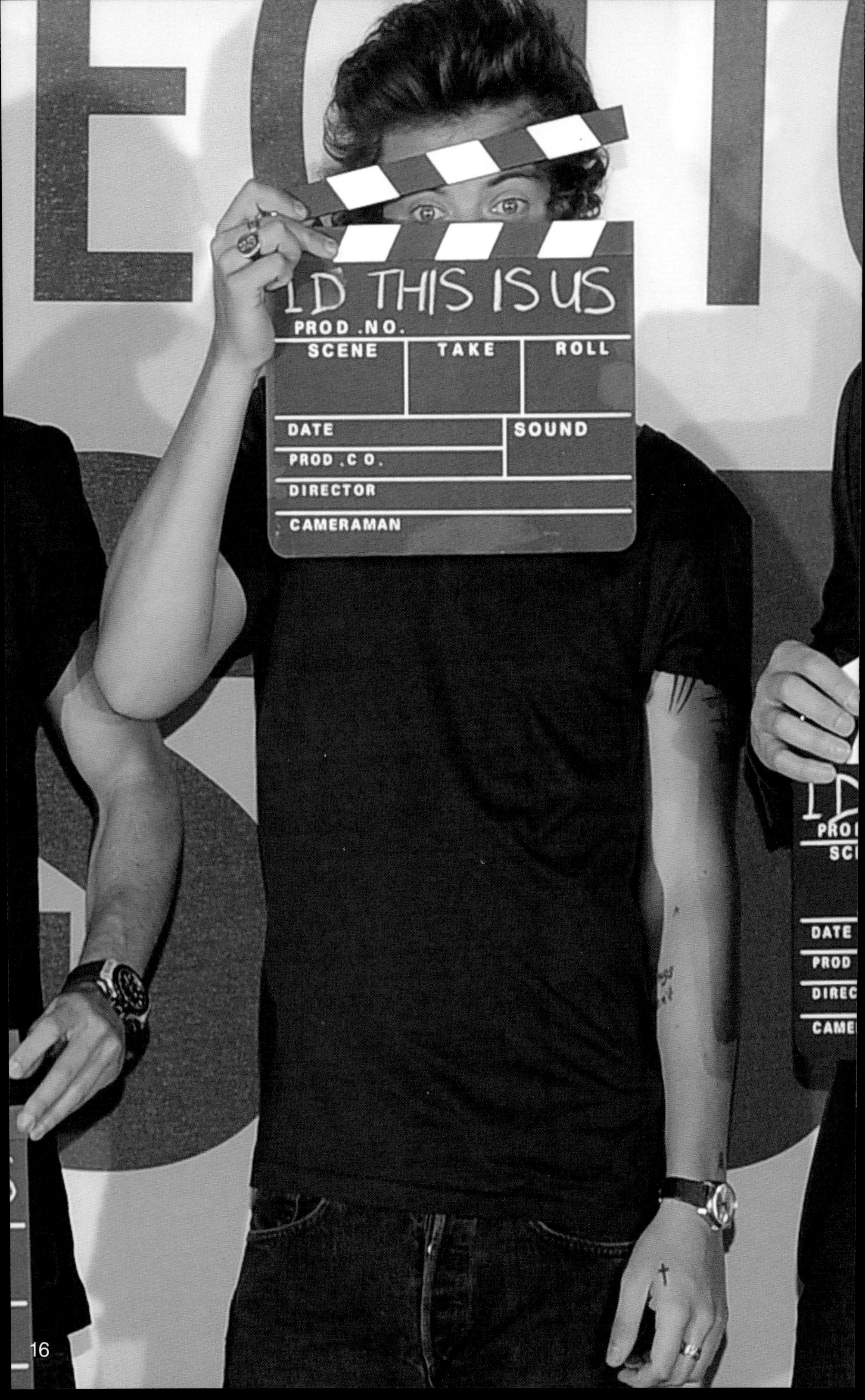
1D THIS IS US
PROD .NO.
SCENE
TAKE
ROLL
DATE
SOUND
PROD .C O.
DIRECTOR
CAMERAMAN

1D go 3D

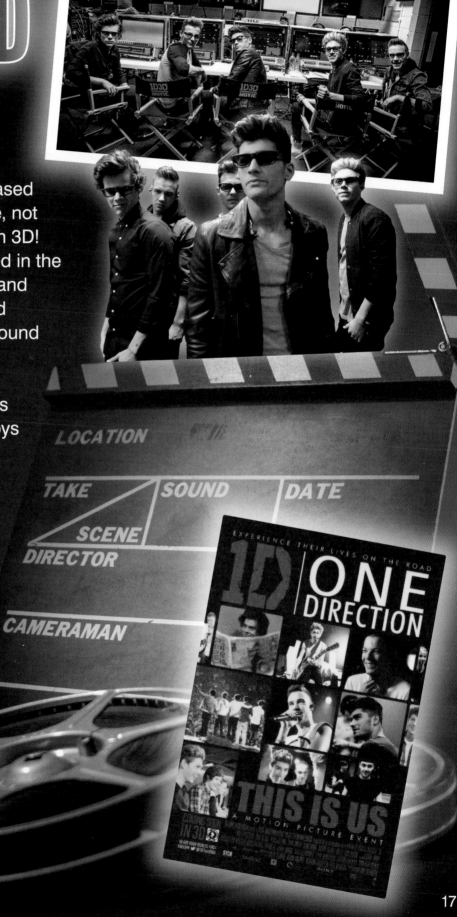

One Direction released their very first movie, not just any movie but in 3D! The movie premiered in the UK on 29th August, and then it was launched around the world around the same time.

'This Is Us' shows us more of what the boys are like in 'real life' when they're hanging out together and when they are on tour or performing. A great way to give fans a glimpse in to their world.

LOCATION

TAKE   SOUND   DATE

SCENE

DIRECTOR

CAMERAMAN

EXPERIENCE THEIR LIVES ON THE ROAD

1D ONE DIRECTION

THIS IS US
A MOTION PICTURE EVENT

COMING SOON
IN 3D

Discography

Harry and the One Direction boys may have only been around for a few years, but they certainly have worked hard in that time, with two albums, 10 singles and 2 tours under their belt already!

Albums

2011

Up All Night

Reached number one in Australia, Canada, Ireland, New Zealand, Sweden and the US. Worldwide sales of over 4.5 million to date.

2012

Take Me Home

Reached number one in UK, Australia, Canada, Ireland, Holland, Belgium, New Zealand, Sweden and the US. Worldwide sales of over 4.4 million to date.

Video Albums

2012

One Direction: Up All Night - The Live Tour

Reached number one in Australia, Canada and the US. Worldwide sales of 1 million to date.

Singles

2010

Heroes

Recorded as part of the X Factor finalists' charity single. Reached number one in UK and Ireland.

2011

What Makes you Beautiful

Number one in UK and Ireland.

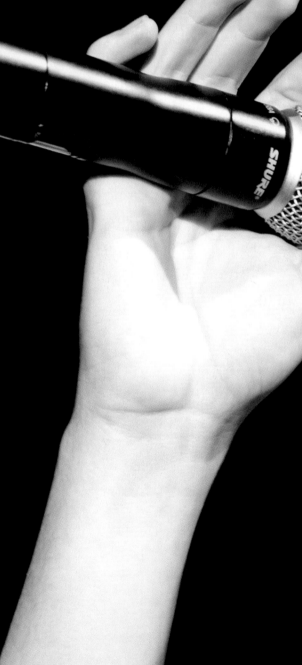

Gotta Be You

Number three in UK and Ireland.

Wishing On A Star

As part of X Factor finalists' single, reached number one in UK and Ireland.

2012

One Thing

Number nine in UK charts.

More Than This

Reached number eighty-six in UK.

Live While We're Young

Number one in Ireland and New Zealand, number three in UK and US.

Little Things

Reached number one in UK.

2013

Kiss You

Number nine in UK charts.

One Way or Another
(Teenage Kicks)

Reached number one in UK, Ireland and the Netherlands.

Best Song Ever

Reached number two in UK, Canada, Denmark and Ireland.

19

CROSSWORD

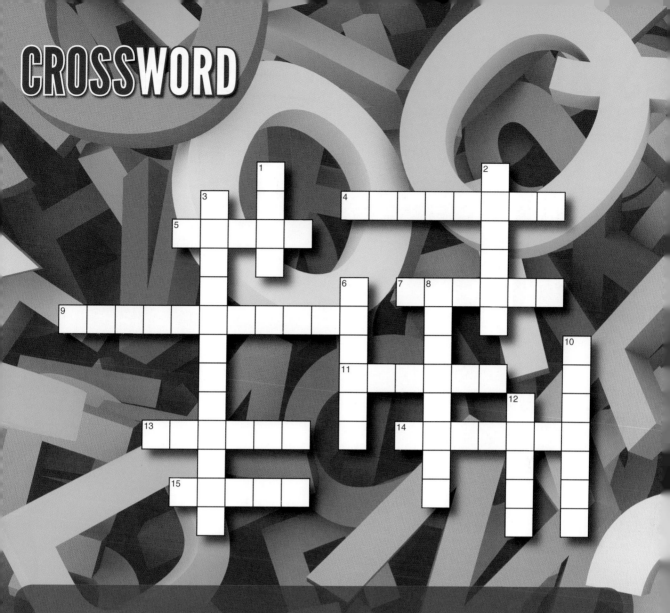

ACROSS

4 Harry hates this red vegetable. (8)
5 Harry shared an apartment with this One Direction member. (5)
7 Harry worked in this kind of shop before the X Factor. (6)
9 Our Harry was lead singer of this chilly band before coming to the X Factor. (5,6)
11 Harry's middle name. (6)
13 Harry has a phobia of these slippery creatures. (6)
14 Harry has four of these, when most of us only have two. (7)
15 Harry's older sister. (5)

DOWN

1 His crowning glory. (4)
2 Harry performed a hit by this legendary singer in his X Factor auditions, Stevie _____. (6)
3 Harry's hometown, in Cheshire. (6,6)
6 One Direction's X Factor mentor, Simon _____. (6)
8 This watery star sign represents Harry's birthday. (8)
10 Harry's hamster was imaginatively called _____. (7)
12 The first song Harry learned the lyrics for was by the King, _____ Presley. (5)

Stage Presence - Live!

23

His real fans

Massages

Harry Loves

His fans and family

Loyalty

Animals

A clean house

Chick flick

Tattoos

Having fun

The rest of the One Direction boys

24

Snakes

Harry doesn't Love

Mayonnaise

Girls who smoke and swear

Olives

Beetroot

People who scream in his face

Anyone who is rude or mean to the rest of the One Direction boys

Styles' *Style*

Ever since he first walked on stage at the X Factor auditions, it was clear that Harry was someone who really liked to make himself look good. Over the years, his love of fashion has really grown, and with the help of stylists and access to great shops all over the world, Harry has started to develop a certain 'look', independent of the other 1D boys. Here is a rundown of some of his (and our) favourite style hits and misses, and his trademarks:

Sunglasses: Harry loves his shades, and prefers classic styles by RayBan.

Hair: You can't talk about Harry's fashion sense without including a mention of his crowning glory. Harry's floppy, curly locks sometimes seem to have a life of their own, despite sometimes being styled into a quiff, they can usually be found scruffily draped over his face. Harry's hair wasn't always curly though - it was straight when he was at Primary school!

Blazers: Harry always looks immaculate on nights out with friends and family. He wears a blazer very well, whether it is wi a nice crisp white shirt or a loose casua t-shirt or vest. He must know this himse as it does seem to be a more favoured item of clothing.

Beanie: On days when his hair isn't quite behaving itself, a beanie comes in very handy at disguising the mess. Harry likes to reach for one of these on his days off, or after a night out on the town.

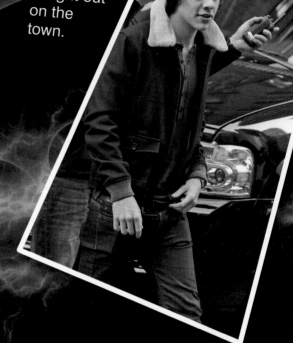

Onesies: Harry and the rest of the 1D boys like to dress up in a cosy onesie every now and again. Just don't wear them outside too often!

Retro t-shirts: Harry rocks the casual look with jeans and a t-shirt. He loves ones with a retro print, especially with a band or album on it – Pink Floyd, The Ramones and Kiss' t-shirts, have all been worn by Harry at some point.

Quiz
20 Questions

1 What is Harry's middle name?

2 What star sign is Harry?

3 What slippery creatures does Harry have a phobia of?

4 Who was Harry's first celebrity crush?

5 What is the name of Harry's home town?

6 Who is the person Harry would most like to duet with?

7 'Isn't She Lovely' is one of the songs Harry sung at X Factor auditions - who is it originally by?

8 Who was the One Direction mentor during X Factor finals?

9 How tall is Harry?

10 Who is Harry's favourite person?

11 Which iconic Liverpool band is Harry a huge fan of?

12 Which ginger-haired songwriter asked Harry to appear in one of his music videos?

13 Harry had a hamster as a pet when he was young - what was it called?

14 Which Canadian rockers gave the first concert Harry attended?

15 What is Harry's motto in life?

16 What is Harry's sister called?

17 What bad habit does Harry hate in a girl?

18 What colour are Harry's eyes?

19 Which global megastar admitted to having a crush on Harry?

20 What does Harry do in his sleep?

Tats What Makes You Beautiful...

Or does it?

Anyone who knows anything about Harry Styles knows that this is a man that loves a bit of ink (well, more than a bit recently!). It seems like Harry's fondness for tattoos is slowly turning into an obsession, with even his bandmates surprised at the speed he gets new ones - in fact Niall even joked and said "Harry seems to have a different one (tattoo) every day!" - dailymail.co.uk

All his inkings have special meaning to the popstar, but we've picked out a small selection of Harry's body art.

17 BLACK – on his chest. This is fictional spy James Bond's lucky gambling number.

A – on his arm. The letter refers to his mum, Anne.

Never Gonna Dance Again - inked on his ankles.

This recent addition to Harry's collection refers to singer George Michael's 1984 hit 'Careless Whisper.'

Gemma – Harry's sister's name is written in Hebrew on his arm.

Swallows – these two birds feature on Harry's upper chest, flying toward each other.

Butterfly – another addition, this time on his torso.

Star – Harry's first tattoo can be found on the inside of his arm to represent each of the five boys of One Direction. It has now been coloured in black.

Won't Stop 'till We Surrender – found next to the star and apparently means that the boys will not break up until they all give up.

Padlock – this little addition was inked by no other than Ed Sheeran.

Ship – on his upper left arm.

Although Harry likes tattoos, they are not for everybody. *Please remember they are permanent and we do not promote or encourage them.*

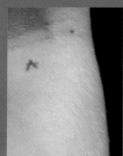
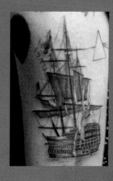
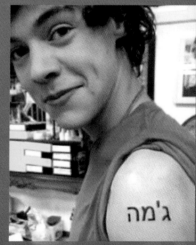
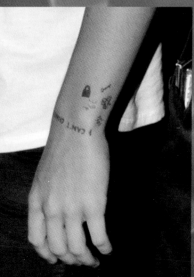

SPOT THE DIFFERENCE

There are ten differences in the image below. Can you spot them all?

Answers on page 61.

Famous Friends

Since he burst out of the X Factor house and into the real world, Harry has certainly made a name for himself as a popular person to have around. Whether at a party, a fashion show, or at the beach, Harry always seems to be having fun with other famous people!

Here are a few of his buddies:

Alexandra Burke: The former X Factor winner has been a big cheerleader for all of One Direction since they appeared on the show, and seems to have a soft spot for our Harry - and who can blame her?

Kimberly Stewart: Harry has been seen leaving Kimberly's house the morning after a party. It was reported that Kimberly - daughter of rock legend Rod Stewart, and Harry shared a dinner date together in LA.

Dionne Bromfield: Soul singer and goddaughter of the late Amy Winehouse, Dionne and Harry have been seen together at Alexandra Burke's birthday party, and sitting in the front row at fashion shows. It looks like the two singers hit it off - only time will tell if anything more than friendship will develop?

Ed Sheeran: Harry is a massive fan of the red-haired singer/songwriter, so much so that Harry agreed to appear in the video for Ed's song 'Drunk'.

Caroline Flack: Harry's super ex - he and Caroline are still great friends and say nice things about each other (in public anyway!).

James Corden: Comedian James and Harry have grown very close over the past few years, and Harry is also close to James's wife Julia and their son Max. Harry was even spotted in New York with the family recently helping them cross the road.

Alain de Botton: Earlier this year, philosopher and all round brainbox Alan Botton tweeted a pic of himself with Harry and posh socialite Jemima Khan, writing alongside the post that the trio talked about (Ancient Greek philosopher) "Plato, Aristotle, love and beauty". Harry quickly followed with a Tweet that read "Socrates, born in Athens in the 5th century BCE, marks a watershed in Ancient Greek philosophy." Who knows where this unlikely pairing will end up, but it's certainly an interesting one to watch! – Twitter.

Nick Grimshaw: Radio 1 DJ, party animal and friend to the stars Nick Grimshaw, is rapidly becoming BFFs with our Harry. Famously, after the 2013 Brits, Nick partied with Harry all night then dragged him into his Radio 1 studio to present the next day's breakfast show - with some funny and some not-so-funny results.

Cara Delevingne: Cara dated Harry briefly, and though they've now split up, he's still friends with the model/all-round posh girl.

Harold Tillman: Retail industry entrepreneur and head of classic British fashion label 'Aquascutum', Harold and Harry have been spotted together at fashion events.

Merchandise Madness

We all love Harry, One Direction, listening to their music and collecting their CDs and posters. But with 1D pop-up stores springing up all over the world, from Glasgow to Philadelphia, it's hard to resist the temptation to collect so much more. Here's just some of the Harry stuff you can buy, it really is merchandise madness and we love it!

T-shirts: There are loads of Harry t-shirts out there, but we love the official 'Future Mrs Styles' ones.

Keychain: The best way to remember to never forget your keys again, is with a mini Harry chain!

Onesie: Harry Styles' Onesie - what better way to snuggle down for a cosy night in?

Toothpaste: Brush your teeth with Harry and the other One Direction boys! It makes going to the dentist much more fun!

Cake topper: He usually looks good enough to eat - well a Styles' cake topper means you can have a slice of Harry anytime you like!

Happy birthday Chloe

Personalised mug: get your own name and message printed on a mug - making your morning cuppa much more refreshing!

Nails: the best manicure you'll ever get - stick these Harry Styles' talons on for a great look!

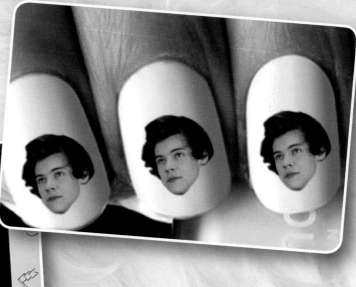

Doll: The likeness isn't exact, but it's still close enough for us. Plus we can say Harry is in our house!

Musical Influences

You can tell Harry loves music, and with a wide variety of tastes, his influences cover a wide range – soul, pop, indie, rock and many more. Here are just some of his favourites...

Elvis Presley: Harry states that Elvis Presley was one of his first musical influences growing up - his parents often played it to him in the car, and Harry has said that the first song he learned the words to was 'The Girl of My Best Friend' by the King.

The Beatles: All of One Direction are fans of the 'Fab Four', with Harry liking them the most. In fact, when he was dating US star – Taylor Swift, it was reported that she was looking to buy him $50k worth of Beatles memorabilia for his Christmas.

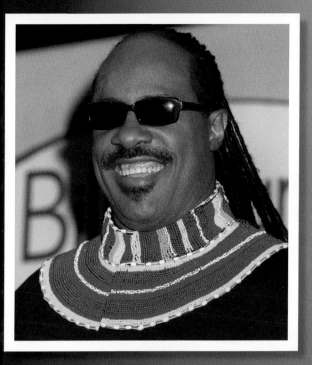

Stevie Wonder: As well as singing the legendary singer's hit 'Isn't She Lovely' at the X Factor auditions, he also sang it at his mum's wedding to stepdad Robin.

Chris Martin: Chris Martin is the one person (alive or dead) that Harry would most like to duet with. When Coldplay sang a line from 'What Makes You Beautiful' at one of their US gigs, Harry was over the moon and tweeted Chris was an "icon".

Aerosmith: Harry tweeted a picture of the album cover for the US rockers 'Greatest Hits' CD, telling the world how much he loves them.

Ed Sheeran: Harry has become friends with the British singer/songwriter, and as well as admiring his work, also agreed to appear in the video for his song 'Drunk'.

Kings of Leon: Harry loves these American rockers and has covered their massive hit 'Use Somebody' on tour.

Seeing DOUBLE!

Harry, along with the other One Direction boys, were immortalised by Madame Tussauds – which they took as a great honour.

Harry's life size waxwork features his trademark suit jacket, skinny jeans and of course big hair!

He said, "We're just kind of a bit overwhelmed. We've been to Madame Tussauds and seen the kind of people who are in there. It's crazy to think that we will be up there with them." – Dailymail.com

The waxworks will have visited London, New York and Sydney, Australia by the end of their travels.

One Harry was good enough, but two? Even better!

Madame Tussauds

New York   Sydney

43

Name That Tune

Let's test your knowledge and see if you can guess which One Direction songs the lyrics below belong to?

1

I promised one day that I'd bring you back a star
I caught one and it burned a hole in my hand, oh
Seems like these days I watch you from afar
Just trying to make you understand
I'll keep my eyes wide open, yeah

2

Do you remember summer '09?
Wanna go back there every night,
Just can't lie, was the best time of my life

3

Show me what you're all about

4

Youth is like diamonds in the sun,
And diamonds are forever.

5

Baby you light up my world like nobody else,
The way that you flip your hair gets me overwhelmed,
But when you smile at the ground it ain't hard to tell

6

Katy Perry's on replay
She's on replay
DJ got the floor to shake, the floor to shake

7

Everyone else can multiply by sixty.
Everyone else can add two

8

You can get, get anything that you want
Baby just shout it out, shout it out
Baby just shout it out, yeah

Answers on page 60.

TWEET TWEET

Harry does like keeping his fans up to date on anything and everything. Here are just some of his many tweets.

@Harry_Styles

Lets go night hiking!!!

Just rode a bicycle round town..got frozen yoghurt and rode back. Nice night.

Just got told that we broke the record? You are all incredible. You keep on surprising us.. Thank youuuu

3 years.. I honestly can't believe it. Thank you so much for everything, we're so lucky to have you. You keep making it more and more fun.

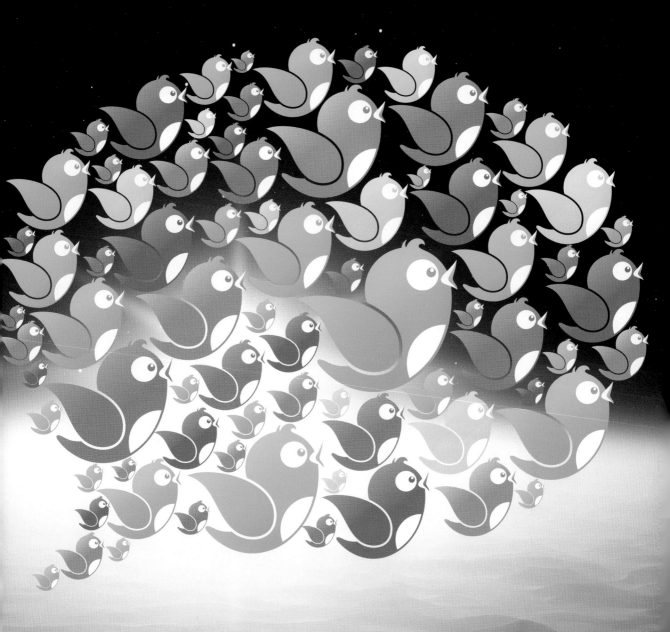

As of this morning, 'Marimba' will never again be my alarm tone.

Does anybody remember green ketchup?

I've always wondered why there's a big line through Harry Potter's birthday cake.

Might go old school and use coloured chocolate wrappers to make some 3D glasses.

Pretty woman is on tv. Wooooooo!

I may or may not have just slipped over getting out the pool.

Always feel lucky when Grease songs come on the radio.

Just had my first ice bath. Note: If someone is laughing as you're getting into something, you probably should stop getting in.

So that's why I have an alarm…

Everyone getting results today, hope you get what you wanted. Good luck with whatever you do next. Life is fun isn't it…

Sign on the side of the road that reads 'I buy houses'. Well done.

Say What?

We could listen to Harry all day!
Here are just a few quotes from the man himself.

Harry has a sensible moment

"I can see how you could get dragged into the bad stuff, but I've got good friends around me, good family. I think I've got my head screwed on." - The Mirror

We'll come on a dinner date with you Harry!

"I'm quite old-fashioned. I like going out to dinner. You have the chance to talk to somebody and get to know them better." - Seventeen

Harry ponders what the future will hold for One Direction

"Naturally I wonder how long it will last. But we get on so well I can't see us having a massive bust-up of anything like that." - The Mirror

Harry on acting his age

"Age is nothing but a number" - We Love Pop

Harry knows who his real, true friends are

"There are always going to be people who are acting like they're better friends with you than they actually are." - We Love Pop

Harry has his priorities right

"You're never going to get used to walking into a room and have people screaming at you. There's a lot of things that come with the life you could get lost in. But you have to let it be what it is. I've learnt not to take everything too seriously." - Vogue

Harry the boy becomes Harry the man

"I feel like I've woken up with suddenly more facial hair and a deeper voice" - Harry's Twitter Feed

C'mon Harry, we think you're pretty cool

"I think you have to be cool to be a good flirt, and I don't think I'm very cool." - The Sun

Anyone like to volunteer?

"I like girls, but I prefer having a girlfriend. I like having someone I can spoil. Somebody to call up in the middle of the night and just talk to. I like getting close to someone like that." – HollywoodLife

Harry on his exhibitionist streak

"Stripping off is very liberating, I feel so free." - sugarscape.com

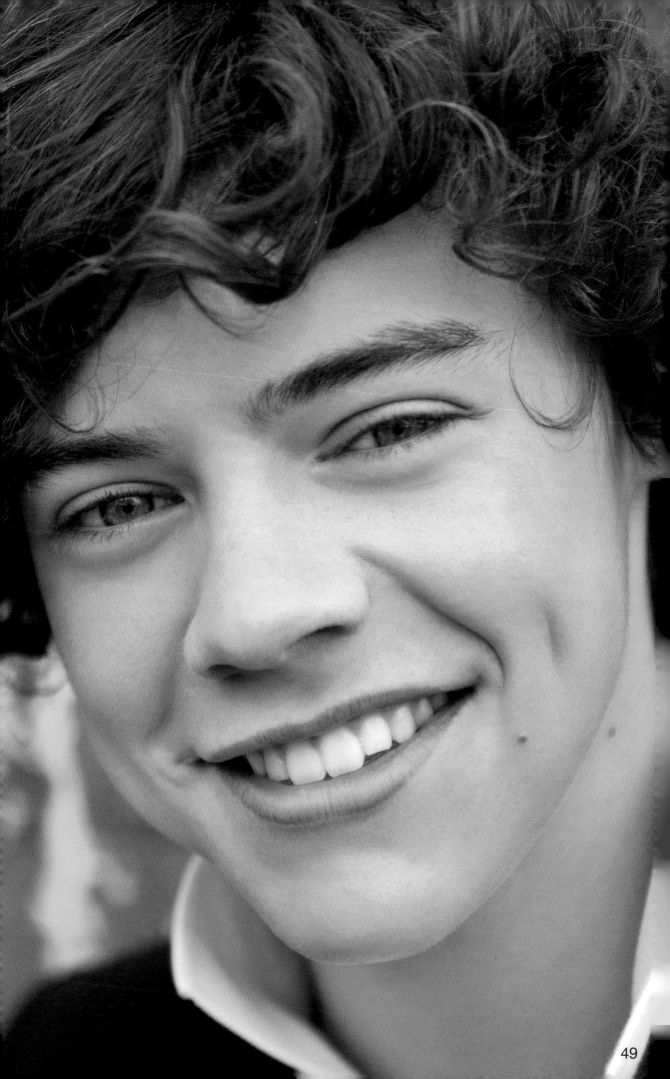

A-Z of Harry Styles

A: Age - despite being the baby of the One Direction boys, Harry has a very wise head on his shoulders.

B: The Beatles - one of Harry's favourite groups, One Direction are now bigger than the fab four in America.

C: Chris Martin - the Coldplay front man is a huge inspiration to our Harry.

D: Directioners - 1D's biggest fans make sure Harry and the boys are supported all over the world.

E: Ed Sheeran - Harry is a huge fan of the singer/songwriter.

F: February 1st - Harry was born on this day in 1994.

G: Gemma - Harry's older sister.

H: Hair - Harry's crowning glory has men and girls jealous of his luscious locks!

I: Isn't She Lovely - Harry sang this Stevie Wonder classic at his X Factor auditions.

J: Juggling - if One Direction split up anytime soon, Harry could take his juggling skills to join the circus instead.

K: Kissing - Harry can often be seen kissing everyone round him - friends, mum, bandmates & fans.

L: Louis Tomlinson - Harry's best pal in the band, the two are often quoted on their 'bromance'.

M: Mum - all good boys love their mother, and Harry is no exception, admitting to calling or texting her up to five times in a day!

N: Nudity - Harry is well known for getting his kit off at any opportunity!

O: One Direction, of course!

P: Pets - Harry loves animals, especially turtles - he even once had a hamster called 'Hamster'.

Q: Quiff - Harry's floppy locks are sometimes styled into a rockabilly quiff, but we prefer the shaggy dog look.

R: Rihanna - the global superstar had admitted to being a fan of the boys, and of Harry especially.

S: Second chances - thank goodness Harry got one on the X Factor.

T: Tattoos - Harry loves a bit of ink, and his latest one has the lyrics from George Michael's 1984 hit 'Careless Whisper' on his ankles.

U: USA - Harry and the One Direction boys have enjoyed massive success in America - being the first British group to go to number one with their debut album.

V: Voice - perfect for making sweet music with.

W: Work hard, play hard, be kind - Harry's motto in life.

X: X Factor - where we first saw Harry perform as a solo artist, then grow into the new group, One DIrection.

Y: Young MIck Jagger - some people think that Harry is the spitting image of the Rolling Stones frontman when he was a young lad, but we're not so sure.

Z: Zzzzz's - Harry loves catching up with his sleep and likes nothing better than a long lie after one of his nights out.

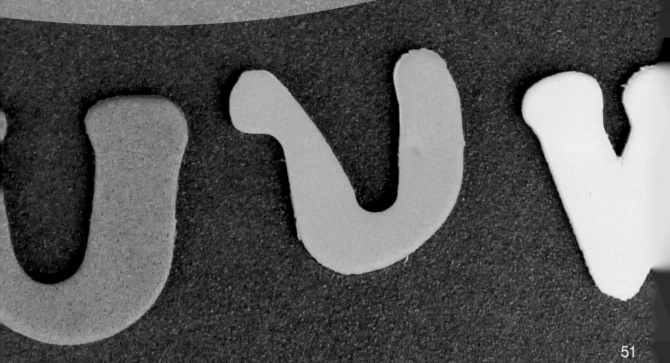

we ♥ love you...

Harry and his Fans

It has to be said that Harry and the rest of the One Direction boys, really do have very loyal fans. From the young to the more mature fan, he bowls everyone over with his charm. Here are a few snaps showing how he takes the time out to have pictures taken, sign autographs and wave to the very people who helped him along the way to becoming a huge star... the fans. Harry really is the best!

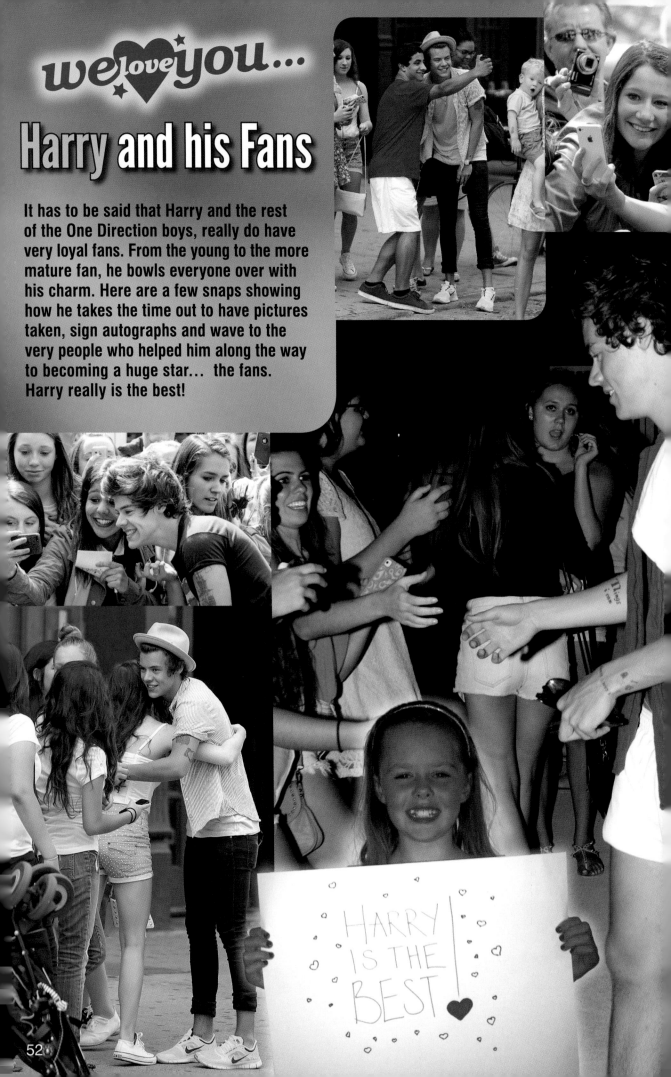

HARRY IS THE BEST ♥

52

Twerk it!

It doesn't take much for Harry to drive his fans wild! A look, a smile, a 'Twerk'?!

In fact he gave us all a treat at the Teen Choice 2013 Awards held in Los Angeles in August, when he was encouraged by his fellow pal in pop - Ed Sheeran, along with the hosts of the award ceremony, to stand up and show off his own 'Twerking' style.

It may have only lasted a few seconds, but it was enough to send the media world into an absolute frenzy! It came as no surprise that the short clip and images of Harry re-creating this new 'dance phenomenon' took no time at all to be circulated around the globe.

Harry himself later tweeted: "Note to self. Don't 'twerk'." Ah Harry, we really didn't mind one bit!

WORDSEARCH

Can you find the fifteen words that are linked to Harry below?
Words can go horizontally, vertically and diagonally in all eight directions.

```
G N I L G G U J S N F N X N
L X X T R D V N M N P F O Q
J N H Z T R B M K I A I X N
T R C M L A N L L C T K N C
W A T J R W Q A T C M L E R
I Z R A N D T O E B L B R S
T Z K V T E R R D E H X M Y
T A K M S T I N W A S L F L
E H A I R D O O H T H R F G
R F J T E H C O J L B W A M
X N M N K T R B T E W L N C
Q F O R X N Q Q X S T M K K
H O L M E S C H A P E L Z H
L L R T V W A C I R E M A P
```

America	Juggling
Beatles	One Direction
Cars	Pilates
Cowell	Snakes
Edward	Tattoo
Hair	Twitter
Hazza	X Factor
Holmes Chapel	

DINNER FOR TWO

Tacos are one of Harry's favourites when it comes to food. If he was coming round for dinner, you'd definitely need this recipe.

Tasty Tacos

Prep time: 5 minutes
Cook time: 16 minutes

Ingredients:
1 lb. ground beef
3 ounces taco seasoning mix
4 taco shells
3/4 cup water
1 cup shredded lettuce
1 cup shredded cheddar cheese
1 cup tomatoes, diced
1 cup taco sauce

Instructions:
Sauté the ground beef in a heavy non-stick pan over a medium to high heat 3-4 minutes, breaking up meat until every piece is browned. Cook through for a further 10-12 minutes on a medium heat, adding in the seasoning and water. Once cooked and seasoned, divide into the taco shells and top with lettuce, cheese and tomatoes. Serve with taco sauce and enjoy!

Optional:
Add some guacamole and sour cream

Top tip:
Harry also loves sweetcorn, so maybe you could add that into the mix too?

Please be very careful when using the cooker, if in doubt get an adult to help you out.

What the Future May Hold

2013 was a huge year for the One Direction boys, and for Harry himself. A few of the things he achieved were - he turned 19, bought an apartment, toured America and set himself on fire on stage (luckily Zayn was there to put out the flames!).

And as the band and Harry himself continue to grow in popularity and confidence, the next few years are bound to be just as busy and exciting for everyone!

Happy 19th Birthday

Tour: In true One Direction style, the boys announced the details of their 'Where We Are' 2014 world stadium tour at Wembley Stadium, where the boys had a kickabout wearing the national football strips of every country they're going to be playing. The tour takes them all over the globe from Chile to Ireland and Brazil to Scotland. They're looking forward to it, but with three UK venues included, it's a fact that we're looking forward to it more!

Solo Album?: It has been reported that Harry has been recording tracks of solo material at a Hollywood studio. We all know that Harry loves the style of music his friend Ed Sheeran makes, so maybe his solo songs are more singer/songwriter than pop classic? Regardless, we'd love to hear them.

More Pictures!: Harry has recently become a favourite of the tabloid paparazzi, who seem to snap him whatever he's doing, from a day out with comedian James Corden and his family, to getting some shopping in. Not that we're complaining about more pictures of the gorgeous one, but it might be nice for Harry to be able to do some things once in a while without a camera going off in his face.

More Tattoos!: We know Harry loves his tattoos, and we know he has a great body, so will he get more? And if so, where? We'll be keeping our eyes out for them.

Success also comes in the form of money - and lots of it in the case of the One Direction boys. Top business analysts have predicted that the boys could become the first ever billion dollar boy band, when you add up the concert ticket sales, record sales, film sales, and of course the all important sales from merchandise. If Harry only gets a fraction of the money that comes to the band in 2014, he's going to be one very rich young man. We hope he manages to use it wisely - we could always suggest a few things to spend it on!

Whatever Harry gets up to in 2014, we know he'll do it in his usual high-energy, enthusiastic manner, with a cheeky grin and a flash of those eyes. We look forward to seeing what the New Year brings for our Harry.

QUIZ ANSWERS

Quiz p.30

1. Edward
2. Aquarius (born February 1st)
3. Snakes
4. Frankie Sanford from The Saturdays
5. Holmes Chapel
6. Chris Martin from Coldplay
7. Stevie Wonder
8. Simon Cowell
9. 5 feet 10 inches
10. His mum Anne
11. The Beatles
12. Ed Sheeran
13. Hamster
14. Nickelback
15. Work hard, play hard, be kind
16. Gemma
17. Swearing
18. Green / blue
19. Rihanna
20. Sleep talk

ANAGRAM p.13

1. One Direction
2. Harry Edward Styles
3. Curly Hair
4. Love Your Mum
5. Very Cute
6. Holmes Chapel
7. Liam Niall Louis Zayn (In any order)
8. Got To Be You

NAME THAT TUNE p.44

1. Don't Let Me Go
2. Rock Me
3. C'mon C'mon
4. Forever Young
5. What Makes You Beautiful
6. Up All Night
7. Your Math Skills Are Terrible/ Maths Song
8. Kiss You

CROSSWORD p.21

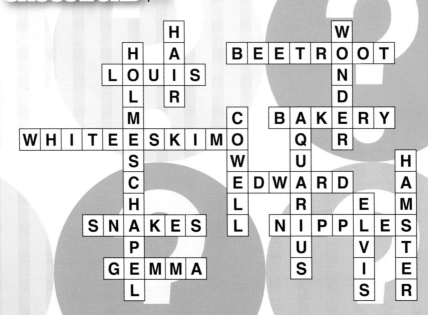

SPOT THE DIFFERENCE p.35

WORDSEARCH p.55

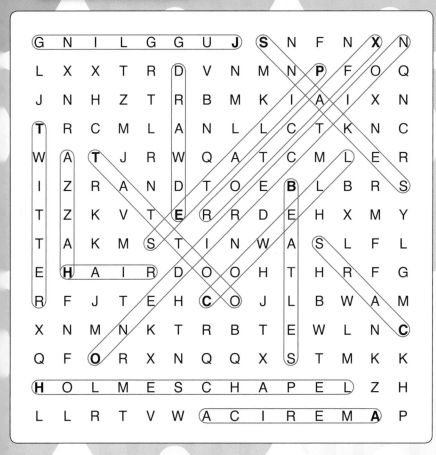

Where's Harry?